The History Teacher's Joke Book
By Richard Di Giacomo

1st Edition © 2012

ISBN 10 098530068X and ISBN 13 9780985300685 $9.99

The History Teacher's Joke Book

2nd Edition © 2015

Table of Contents:

Acknowledgements

I would like to dedicate this book to Ronald Reagan. He was my favorite president and by far one of the best joke tellers to ever hold the office. I would also like to thank Aaron Willis and others at Social Studies School Service for helping me to first get my books distributed to the educational market, and Nina Linebaugh and others at Teacher's Discovery for their enthusiastic support for my books. Special thanks go to James Dewitt, a former student who first gave me the "Worst Joke Award". This has prompted countless students to ask me, "Which joke earned the award for you?" My standard reply has always been, "It wasn't any one joke, but rather a systematic torture of my students throughout the year." This is born out by the fact that the most frequent comment I get in my course evaluations is "Great class; crummy jokes!" (Along with comments like "How about if you didn't give any tests?" or "Too bad we can't watch a movie every day."). Finally, I would like to thank my students for putting up with my horrible puns and corny jokes. Without their sighs, moans, and blank stares I would have never known which of this material was good and which wasn't. I hope that these jokes add a little excitement to your classes and help students to have fun with history. I apologize in advance for any intentional anachronisms, misspellings and material accidentally "borrowed" from other comics. It was all done in good fun.

Chapter One: Geography

Asia

Moe: "Do you know a good Middle Eastern Joke?"
Joe: "Iraq my brains trying to think of one, but I can't."
Moe: "That was so bad Iran away."
Joe: "Kuwait to get started."
Moe: "You can't be Syrias?"
Joe: "Was that a bad joke? I'm Saudi."
Moe "Yemen to that!"
Joe: "Oman, please stop it!"

Doris: "Why is there never any precipitation in the Arabian Desert?"
Boris: "Because they always say, 'Bahrain!'"

Sally: "My father left his suitcase at the Iraqi airport."
Allie: "What did you do?"
Sally: "I told him, 'Hey, you left your Baghdad!'"

Sue: "Who is always in a hurry?"
Drew: "The Russians!"

Waldo: "Where is Indochina?"
Aldo: "Right on the other side of outdo' (outdoor) China."

Dee: "Are you from Thailand?"
Lee: "Yes, Siam."

Tina: "Do you want to hear a Laosy joke?"
Dina: "No, you are Mekong enough bad ones already!"

Alfie: "How do you tie your shoes in China?"
Ralphie: "First Taiwan, and then the other."

Millie: "If you don't get rich singing in Malaysia what do you do?"
Willie: "Go to Singapore."
Rob: "What did one Chinese dairy farmer say to the other?"
Bob: "I don't know."
Rob: "Stay away from Macao!"

Andy: "What is your worst travel experience?"
Candy: "One time I barely got out of Burma."
Andy: "What a close shave!"

Art: "Where do they cook the best Southern cooking in Asia?"
Bart: "In Korea, they have lots of Seoul food."

Mitch: "Why does the Dalai Lama go to Las Vegas?"
Rich: "He loves Tibet!"

Dora: "What do you say to all of the highest hills in Russia?"
Nora: "Ural Mountains."

Shawna: "What's the biggest wound in India?"
Donna: "Mysore."

Ed: "What do you do if your food store flops in India?"
Fred: "Open a New Delhi."

Sal: "What do you do if the government falls in Afghanistan?"
Al: "Kabul together another one."

Kay: "What the easiest job in Afghanistan?"
Fay: "Being a mountain guide; it's a Kush job."

Kyle: "What do you do if your friend Stan can't make it on a trip to Asia?"

Lyle: "Don't Pakistan."
Kyle: "Could you hide him in a blanket?"
Lyle: "Sure, just Afghanistan."

Sancho: "Why is Jordan so well defended?"
Pancho: "Because they will defend it to Amman."

Kelly: "What do Indian pilots do in combat?"
Nelly: "Open the Bombay doors."

Fred: "The biggest volcanic explosion in Indonesia was at Mount Krakatoa."
Ned: "Hmm, sounds like something a chiropractor worked on."

Bill: "I heard that the government of the Philippines is trying some new reforms." Jill: "Yeah, those guys in Manila are always pushing the envelope."

Jane: "What don't you like about Vietnam?"
Lane: "The government in Vietnam can really Hanoi me."

Kim: "Is that woman from the Philippines nice?"
Jim: "Yeah, she is a regular Leyte."

When Mongolians walk they like to take big steppes.

When you see Tigris are Euphrates?

If a sea captain doesn't like Sri Lanka, he can just Ceylon by.

A businessman who wanted more ties bought some in Thailand where ties are very collar full.

Oceania

Mike: "Why do Hindu priests do so well in Australia?"
Ike: "They kangaroo anywhere they want."

Steve: "Why was that guy from Darwin such a failure?"
Terri: "I heard he really made a monkey out of himself."

Mick: "What's Christmas like in Australia?"
Nick: "I hear they have plenty of reefs hanging around."

Bess: "Why are you leaving Australia?"
Jess: "I Canberra no more."

Tammy: "Where are the wisest people on earth?"
Sammy: "The Solomon Islands."

Bill: "Why didn't you leave the South Pacific sooner?"
Phil: "I couldn't Marshall enough strength."

Hank: "Where do people like to talk a lot?"
Frank: "Yap Island."

Minnie: "Have you been to Bikini Atoll?"
Winnie: "No, it just doesn't suit me."

Danny: "I like the mammals in Tasmania."
Annie: "You devil, you!"

Pat Sajak told her not to turn that letter. Vanuatu know better!

Things made in Australia are high koala-ty.

 Africa

Scott: "What kinds of cars do they drive in Khartoum?"
Dott: "4-door Sudans."

Larry: "What is the favorite TV channel in Sudan?"
Sherry: "The Khartoum network."

Brent: "Can ships talk in Egypt?"
Kent: "I don't know, but I know what the Port Said."

Theo: "What's the only bird on the Nile River?"
Leo: "Aswan."

Tricia: "Kenya name a country in East Africa?"
Leticia: "Yes. Why, Uganda go there some day?"

Billy: "Why did you sail north of Madagascar?"
Tilly: "I wanted to collect Seychelles on the seashore."

Bart: "What is Superman's favorite city in Africa?"
Art: "Capetown."

Flo: "What is your geometry teacher's favorite country in Africa?"
Moe: "Angola."

Harry: "Have you been to Brazzaville?"
Mary: "No, I've been busy."
Harry: "Oh come on, you Congo there anytime you want."

Hazel: "What is the favorite name for boys in Central Africa?"
Basil: "Chad."

Fern: "Why do they have trouble voting in N'djamena?"
Vern: "There are too many hanging Chads on the ballots."

Kim: "What's the fastest growing city in Africa?"
Tim: "Tripoli."

Jan: "What is the favorite building toy in Nigeria?"
Fran: "Lagos."

Jake: "Where is the best fast food in Africa?"
Blake: "Togo."

Lana: "What is the best sport among the Berbers?"
Juana: "Rugby."

May: "Which canned fish is the favorite in North Africa?"
Tray: "Tunis."

Cassie: "Where is the best place to look up travel directions in
Africa?
Blanca: "The Atlas Mountains."

Birdie: "Where can you find cheap singers in Africa?"
Kitty: "The Canary Islands."
Birdie: "Sounds pretty cagey to me."

Show me someone in denial and I'll show you a person in
Egypt up to his ankles.

When there are auto accidents in Sudan the vehicles go the
Khartoum.

Have you Benin Dahomey since the name changed?
Are you Ghana go to Accra?

The environmentalist decided to buy an electric car because

he was Madagascar (mad at gas car).

 Europe

Lynn: "Where do most of the barbers in Europe come from?"
Flynn: "Poland."

Monica: "How fast do you drive in Norway?"
Veronica: "Oslo." (oh, slow).

Myron: "What happens to fires in Switzerland?"
Byron: "They just Bern and Bern."
Loretta: "What's the best smelling city in Europe?"
Concetta: "Cologne."

Hanz: "How is life in Hamburg these days?"
Franz: "Oh, you know the same old grind."

Clair: "I heard you got a job in Frankfurt."
Blair: "Hot dog!"

Pierre: "What is the biggest cat in France?"
Robert: "Lyon."

Sean: "I heard you opened a window shop in Scotland."
John: "How did the Glasgow?"

Geoffrey: "How can you say, 'Long live the Prince.' in the UK?"
Chelsea: "God save the Wales!"

Claudette: "Have you been to the Riviera?"
Monette: "No, but I hear the beaches are Nice."

Anna: "What is the favorite dessert in Valletta?"
Stefana: "Malted shakes."

Daniele: "What were you doing in Italy's capital?"
Michele: "Oh, just Roman around."

Zoe: "What is the favorite name for girls in Bulgaria?"
Chloe: "Sofia."

Those who jump off a Paris bridge are in Seine.

Italian building inspectors in Pisa are leanient.

In a Scandinavian race the last Lapp crossed the Finnish line.

The Irish should be rich because their capital is always Dublin.

Britain is a wet place since the queen has had a long reign.

I Czeched on the Prague-ress of my geography.

If you Russia round and Ukraine your neck don't Crimea river.

People have a happy time vacationing in Ireland because they are walking on
Eire.

Television sets in Britain have to cross the English Channel.

People in Switzerland can't learn to ski without a lot of Alp.

A new country in Europe decided to conduct a flag poll.

If you lose your library book in Romania, do the police issue a Bucharest?

Do music teachers in Yugoslavia give you a Belgrade?

I like European food so I decided to Russia over there because I was Hungary. After Czech'ing the menu I ordered Turkey fried in Greece. When I was Finnished I told the waiter 'Spain good but there is Norway I could eat another bite!'"

Latin America

Cecilia: "How's the weather in Santiago?"
Ofelia: "Oh, a little Chile."

Pamela: "Did you get a job in Lima?"
Angela: "Yes but the pay wasn't worth beans."

Miguel: "Can you name a neighbor of French Guiana?"
Manuel: "Suriname one."

Ricardo: "Does he know that British Honduras changed its name?"
Gerardo: "Yes, he Belize so."

Hernando: "Did you enjoy your vacation to Chihuahua?"
Fernando: "Yes, but I am a little dogged."

Miles: "I got a job in Kingston."
Giles: "Great! Jamaica lot of money?"

Reginald: "Did you enjoy your trip to the Bahamas?"
Archibald: "Nassau it all already."

Lisette: "What countries do lovers avoid?"
Antoinette: "Haiti."

Barry: "Where is the best place in Central America to send a SWAT team?"
Kerry: "The Mosquito Coast."

Mother: "Andrew, what makes you think that you own all of the mountains in South America?"
Andrew: "Mom, you said they were all Andes."
Kenny: "Can you help me get ready for my trip to the Andes?"
Jenny: "Sure, alpaca suitcase for you."

Gloria: "What are the luckiest cards in South America?"
Doria: "The Straits of Magellan."

Beth: "What's the best movie location in South America?"
Seth: "Montevideo."

Paolo: "What is the number one product of Brazil?"
Salvador: "Brazilians!"

Esther: "What is the favorite island for bunnies?"
Bunny: "Easter Island."

Luz: "What is the favorite souvenir toy for Tibetans who visit the Andes?"
Cruz: "Dolly llamas."

Teacher: "Which South American country has the strictest judges?"
Wise guy: "I heard that in Ecuador there is very little latitude."

Kim: "What did one animal say to the other when he nervously crossed the Amazon River?"
Tim: "I don't see any piranhas. What's eating you?"

Visitors to Cuba are usually Havana good time.

If you said you were from South America, I would not Bolivia.

I got a bang out of my trip to Grenada.

If you are planning a trip to South America, Easter Island is a place where you can get a big head start.

North America

Herbert: "Did they ever find gold in Canada?"
Albert: "Yukon bank on that!"

Micky: "Ready? Alaska question."
Vicky: "Sure, but Juneau the answer?"

Victoria: "How much land was left for the Eskimos in Canada?"
Gloria: "Practically Nunavut".

Bonnie: "Where do you go to see picture perfect scenery?"
Connie: "Kodiak Island."

Chuck: "What happens when you tee off well in Manitoba?"
Huck: "Nothing, you just Winnipeg."

Bruce: "I heard they have a new sports team in Quebec."
Luce: "Yeah, they Ottawa the competition."

Cal: "What happens if you lose your keys in Eastern Canada."
Hal: "You better get a Labrador retriever!"

Brian: "Why is it so hard to catch a fish in Prince Albert?"
Ryan: "Haven't you heard?   It takes Saskatchewan!"

Nancy: "In which state do they do the most laundry?"
Clancy: "It's got to be Washington!"

Ruth: "Who is the noisiest mother in Washington?"
Booth: "Yakima."

Bunny: "What's the tallest juvenile delinquent in Oregon?"
Sonny: "Mount Hood."
Selma: "What's the proudest town in California?"
Thelma: "Fort Bragg."

Dirk: "What's the shiest city in California?"
Kirk: "Modesto."

Son: "Dad, can you name any cities in Arizona?"
Father: "I can name Tuscon."

Troy: "Did you strike oil in your well in Nevada?"
Roy: "No, all I did was Winnemucca."

Denise: "What's the funniest cactus in the Southwest?"
Patrice: "Yucca, yucca, yucca."

Mark: "What's the spookiest town in Wyoming?"
Clark: "Casper."

Tom: "Is the scenery nice in Montana?"
Dom: "Yep, it's a Butte!

Bobbie: "Where do most of the lawyers live in Iowa?"
Robbie: "Sioux City."

Hailey: "Which crime has the lowest penalty in Oklahoma?"
Bailey: "Panhandling."

Don: "What's the unhappiest place in the Midwest?"
Juan: "The state of Missouri."

Chris: "Which state is mentioned in the Bible?"
Kris: "Noah looked out of the Arkansas dry land."

Teri: "Where are the smallest fruits in Minnesota?"
Terry: "Minneapolis."

Wayne: "Where is the most wedding food served in Illinois?"
Lane: "Decatur."

Tricia: "What is the favorite pastime of teenagers in Ohio?"
Trisha: "Dayton."

Brad: "What do zookeepers say in Michigan?"
Chad: "Kalamazoo, the animals all escaped."

Preston: "What's the best place to discover in Ohio?"
Weston: "Columbus."

Bernardo: "Which area in Mississippi do elephants hate?"
Eduardo: "Tuscaloosa."

Kelly: "How's your new life in Georgia?"
Shelly: Oh, I'm Macon a living."

Jerry: "What do lovers do in Florida?"
Shari: "Daytona Beach."

Maureen: "Did you get to see much of Virginia?"
Doreen: "No, Chesapeake."

Mavis: "What happens when the buildings all get full in
Maryland."
Davis: "They just Baltimore."

Megan: "What's the most alert state?"
Regan: "Delaware."

Mel: "Where are the most talented felines in New York?"
Del: "The Catskills."

Merry: "Where do they eat the most fish in Pennsylvania?"
Perry: "Altoona."

Merle: "What do they do with their boats in Massachusetts?"
Pearl: "Salem, of course."

Mia: "Why do some people have trouble writing essays in New England?"
Tia: "They have trouble coming up with a Maine idea."

Is the Fort Worth much any more in Texas?

Chapter Two: World History

Ancient History

Did ancient Mesopotamians go on a Sumer vacation?

Matt: "My teacher said that the priests made burnt offerings to the gods on altars atop the temples in Mesopotamia."
Pat: "Yes, that's true, but didn't your mom tell you its wrong to smoke Ziggurats?"

First Student: "I heard that the Babylonians talked a lot."
Second Student: "Its true; they would just Babylon and on."

Annie Tolia: "Why did the priests of Mesopotamia lose their train of thought?"
Baby Lon: "Because they always said, 'Ur, let me see...'"

Persian: "Which ancient people had the best news?"
Kitty: "It must have been Media."

Marduk: "Which ancient people were always in a rush?"
Tiamat: "The Hurrians."

David: "Who were the proudest ancient people?"
Jonathon: "The Hatti?"

The pharaohs of Egypt worked out the first pyramid scheme.

Teacher: "Sometimes pharaohs died quite young."
Student: "Tut, tut, what a shame!"

Rose: "Why was Mother's day so popular in ancient Egypt?"
Etta: "Because everyone loves their mummy!"

Mame: "Which ancient king had the easiest job?"
Luke: "Must have been the Kingdom of Kush."
Cleopatra lived in a state of denial.

Alfie: "Why did the Phoenicians leave their homeland?"
Betty: "Sooner or later you would Tyre of it too."

Ahab: "What happens when Solomon gets tired of his beer?"
Jezebel: "Hebrews another."

Wow, that guy is so old he has been around since the Dead
Sea was sick.

There is some Confucion about the oldest religion in China.

Did you know that donuts were first made in Greece?

Brutus: "Caesar had some difficulty conquering the area that is
modern day France."
Cassius: "Those people had some Gaul!"

Diana: "The great warrior Achilles thought he was invincible."
Hermes: "What a heal!"

Greek Slave: "Master Playwright, what do you do want me to
do with these bad rough drafts?"
Playwright: "Euripides, I don't want to keep them anymore."

Ares: "What happens when a Greek warrior stubs his toe?"
Aphrodite: "I guess that makes him Hoplite from then on."

You could always count on Ajax to scrub up the competition.

Many stories by the Greeks have been myth-interpreted.

Darius: "Why did Alexander the Great replace his father as king?"
Roxanne: "He just couldn't Phillip the empire any further."

Zeus: "Why was Alexander successful at solving the Riddle at Gordium?"
Hera: "Because he wasn't a knotty boy."

Apollo: "Which ancient battle had the best lunch meat?"
Vulcan: "The Battle of Salamis."

When Julius first saw his wife, did he Caesar?

Julius: "Why would it be easy to be a newspaper writer in ancient Rome?
Antony: "I don't know, why?"
Julius: "Because everyone would like to see your columns!"
Teacher: "The Romans were a very war-like people."
Wiseguy: "I guess that Mars their reputation."

Romulus: "Why did Roman speakers have such an easy time persuading an audience?"
Remus: "Because they were all forum!"

Elijah: "Who was the shortest Hebrew prophet?"
Elisha: "Nehemiah."

Moses: "Which Biblical hero was an orphan?"
Aaron: "Joshua, son of Nun."

Peter: "How did Judas end his career?"
Paul: "Oh nothing, he was just hanging around."

Paul: "What kinds of games did the Romans play?"
Silas: "I don't know, but I heard that the Saints lost to the Lions a lot."

Barbara: "What was the richest Barbarian tribe?"
Frank: "The Alamanni."

Jay: "Which enemy of Rome would have made the best computer graphic artists?"
Peg: "The Picts."

Angle: "Which Barbarian tribe would have made the best grocery store baggers?"
Saxon: "The Vandals; they sacked all of Rome."

Medieval Times

Charlemagne was the best king of Western Europe, to be perfectly Frank.

Pepin: "Which Medieval king smelled the best?"
Charles: "Charlemagne, he often lived in Cologne."

Teacher: "Why were the Vikings so tough?"
Wiseguy: "They could always horn in on the competition."

Noble: "What did lords say when their peasants revolted near the beach?"
Peasant: "Serfs up!"

Leo: "What did the Pope serve on a hot day?"
Benedict: "Popesicles."

Arthur: "What was the favorite sport of knights?"
Guinevere: "Jousting, because they liked to Lancelot."

Sire: "Did knights ever fight in the desert?"
Knave: "Probably, they liked to go to Camelot."

Teacher: "Sometimes the archers ran out of arrows or had no place to store them during battle."
Wiseguy: "I quiver to think about it."

Crossbows fired either a bolt or an arrow, but no matter what you call it, that's nothing to quarrel about.

Helmut: "Why did knights like to hang out together in their armor?"
Dirk: "They wanted to have some mail bonding."

Percival: "Why did knights send their sons to live with another knight's family?"
Gawain: "They wanted them to be on the same page."

Professor: "It was easy to hurt a knight in the legs."
Armorer: "That really greaves me!"

Count: "What could you say if a man from Czechoslovakia wore an old suit of armor?"
Countess: "The Czech is in the mail!"

Bocaccio: "Professore Alighieri, what was it like writing your book?
Dante: "It was pure hell!"

Sister Elizabeth: "Why did medieval nuns never change their outfits?"
Sister Mary Margaret: "They were afraid it could be habit-forming."

Teacher: "Of course, you know, there weren't really any dragons in the Middle Ages."
Wiseguy: "Yes, but I know how they got dragon milk."
Teacher: "Really, how?"
Wiseguy: "All you need is a cow with only three legs!"

Teacher: "The life of a hermit contained many deprivations."
Wiseguy: "Yes, I'm sure there was plenty to crab about."

The Renaissance

Lucrezia: "Why did Michelangelo quit working on his 17th church?"
Cesare: "He had to finish the Sistine Chapel."

Donatello: "Why did Galileo quit medical school?"
Rafaello: "He decided to drop everything and study gravity."

Archie: "Joan of Arc had a lot at stake."
Fletcher: "I guess you could say she really had her career go up in smoke!"
Archie: "Yeah, that really burns me up!"

Monty: "Why did Aztec priests do so well?"
Zuma: "Because they were willing to sacrifice anything for their career."

Fran: "What would Jimmy Durante sing if he were with Pizzaro?"
Cisco: "Inca, a-dink, an Inca-a dink-a-doo!"

Lorenzo: "What did Machiavelli and a bad photo developer have in common?"

Cosimo: "They both never got to see the prints (Prince) develop."

Teacher: "What was the first bus in America?
Class clown: "The Columbus."

Teacher: "What would have happened if the Spanish Armada had been smaller?
Class clown: "They would have called it the Spanish Armadillo?"
When the Russians finally defeated the Mongols they had established Tartar control.

Student: "Did Martin Luther lose a lot of weight?"
Teacher: "What makes you say that?"
Student: "Well, you said that he went through the Diet of Worms!"

Student: "Did Martin Luther breed a lot of cattle?"
Teacher: "What makes you say that?"
Student: "Well, you said that he was given a Papal bull!"

During the Renaissance, Francis Bacon had some sizzling new ideas about science.

Professor: "We all know that Vesalius had a few skeletons in his closet."
Student: "Yes, but he built up a great body of evidence to prove his points about anatomy."
Professor: "I guess you could say he was a real cut up!"

Sammy: "What would Rene Descartes have said if he were a skunk?"
Tammy: "I stink; therefore I am."
Holly: "I heard they are coming out with a new movie about pirates."

Woody: "Oh really, what is it rated?"
Holly: "RRRRRRR!"

William: "What do cavemen and the actors of the Globe Theatre have in common?"
Elizabeth: "They both got to shake spear."

The Age of Revolutions

Teacher: "Which thinker was the key to understanding the Enlightenment?"
Know-it-all: "John Locke."

Teacher: "What was Isaac Newton's famous relative?"
Wiseguy: "Fig?"

Teacher: "What was Adam Smith's famous relative?"
Wiseguy: "Up?"
Teacher: "What?"
Wiseguy: "That way their mother could call them together 'up and at'em'."

Teacher: "I hear that the guillotine was a real pain in the neck."
Wiseguy: "Yeah, but it was nothing to lose your head over!"
Teacher: "Chop, chop! Moving right along."
Wiseguy: "You're such a cutup!"

I guess that Marie Antoinette proved that you can't have your cake and eat it too.

A grenade thrown into a kitchen in France would result in Linoleum Blownapart.

Don: "Who was the best bowler in Latin America?"
Juan: "Simon Bowlivar."

Ever since Paul went on that midnight ride we will Revere his name.

Colonial news reporter: "While jeering insults to the traitor Arnold, the crowd eggs Benedict".

The Continental Congress called on Betsy Ross because support for the revolution was flagging.

Teacher: "How do we know that Napoleon was good with cannons?"
Wiseguy: "Because otherwise he would have been known as Napoleon Blownapart!"

Teacher: "Can an obscure figure from a small Mediterranean island become the Emperor of all France?"
Class: "Of Corsican!"

Teacher: "Why didn't the British send the entire fleet to meet the French at the Battle of Trafalgar?"
Wiseguy: "I guess that they thought they could wrestle with the French navy with a half Nelson!"

Teacher: "Why did Napoleon return from exile and try lead France into war again?"
Wiseguy: "I guess that he felt that he needed some more Elba room."

Benjamin Franklin: "Thomas, have we gotten our independence yet?"
Thomas Jefferson: "By George, I think we have got it!"

The Industrial Revolution

Watt was the name of the inventor of the steam engine?

Teacher: "Who was the inventor of the telephone?"
Smartypants: "I don't know but his name rings a bell."

Teacher: "The early inventors of the railroad really had a hard time getting their project on track."
Wiseguy #1: "I'll bet that really got them steamed up!"
Teacher: "You're making me lose my train of thought."
Wiseguy # 2: "Don't have such a one-track mind."

Student: "I can't remember his name, but Lincoln's successor wasn't as good of a president as he was."
Professor: "I'll Grant you that."

Lecturer: "After winning a strike for seamstresses the union leader said, "Sew on, and sew forth!'"
Wiseguy #1: "I'll bet that left the crowd in stitches."
Wiseguy #2 "Sometimes the situation is not all that it seams."
Lecturer: "Their strike was a thimble of their oppression."
Wiseguy #2:"Quit needling me."

Instructor: "Why did Standard Oil know so much about geology?"
Wiseguy: "Because their founder was a Rocky feller."

Student: "The famous Indian fighter really should be known as General Custard."
Instructor: "Why?"
Student: "He got his just desserts."

Teacher: "Why did Theodore Roosevelt drop out of politics?"
Smart Alec: "Because Teddy could bear no more."

Did Sigmund's daughter wear a Freudian slip?

Teacher: "What did Bessemer say when he found a better fuel for his converter?"
Wise guy: This coke is the real thing!
Teacher: "Ha, ha. Did that allow him to steel an advantage over the competition?"

Thomas Edison finished the phonograph in record time.

Teacher: "George Eastman invented the camera just to see what would develop."
Wise guy #1: "I shutter to think what the world would be like without it."
Wise guy #2: "I guess that lens even more honor to his name."
Teacher: "Let's try to keep this discussion in focus."

The Age of Imperialism

Instructor: "Which colonial war interested the British the least?"
Wiseguy: "The Boer War."

If you were sailing on the Vaal River for a long time some one was bound to say, "Bechuanaland here."

Teacher: "Class, do you know where Djibouti is?"
Wiseguy: "Wasn't there a disco song called 'Shake Djibouti'?"

By capturing the Bengal, the British thought they could really catch India by the tail.

The Americans already had some Pacific Islands, so they thought they would take Samoa.

Stanley: "Have you seen Victoria Falls?"
Livingston: "Yes. Don't worry, she gets back up again."

Mussolini: "What did the Italy say after their defeat at Adua?"
Badoglio: "Abyssinia later!"

Mahdi: "How did Lawrence of Arabia teach the Arab tribal leaders to dance?"
Mullah: "Sheik to sheik."

WWI

Teacher: "Most of the fighting took place on the Western Front."
Know-it-all: "It must have been Somme battle!"

The German navy was really sub-standard.

The Ottoman Empire tried to couch their surrender in the best terms possible.

Teacher: "What was the British response to the German trenches?
Pupil: "Tanks a lot!"

Francis: "What kind of transportation were the Turks lacking?"
Ferdinand: "The Otto, man."

After von Richtofen was shot down, The Germans were Baron of good flying aces.

Willy: "Why did the Allies fight so hard on the Western Front?"
Nicky: "Because there was so much to Loos."

The French just bubbled with excitement at the opportunity to attack the Germans at Champagne.

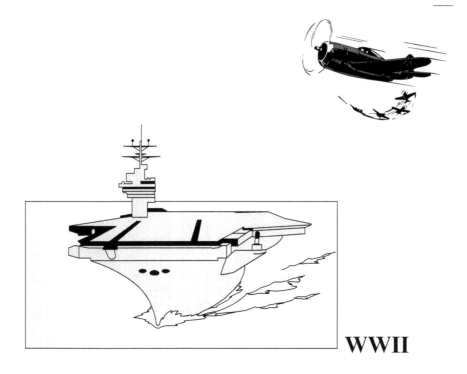

WWII

The Warsaw a quick defeat for Poland.

Terrel: "What did Churchill say to the Soviet ambassador?"
Darrell: "Quit Stalin and join the Allies."

Winston: "What was the British Navy's favorite cereal in WWII?"
Franklin: "Malta meal."

The resistance to Russia in Scandinavia would fight on to the Finnish.

Adolf: "What kind of shoes did American tank drivers have to wear?"
Eva: "Patton leather."

Monty: "Why did the British send tanks to reinforce

Egypt?"
Ike: "Tobruk the German advance."

Harry: "What do dieters and the Allies in WWII have in common?"
Bess: "They both have to go through the Battle of the Bulge."

Franklin: "Why was it so hard for Japanese pilots to get dates?"
Eleanor: "Because the girls thought they were a bunch of flying zeroes."

The Japanese thought that if they could win at Pearl Harbor, the World would be their oyster.

FDR: "What would a computer tell you if you asked it if Germany could win WWII?"
Uncle Joe: "Axis denied."

Tojo: "What do you get when you cross a rock concert and D-day?"
Hirohito: "Operation Overloud."

WWII oxymorons:
French defense.   Russian war plans.
American preparedness.   Italian strategy.
Japanese victory conditions. British gains.   German ally.
Kamikaze roundtrip.   Stalin's lifelong friend.

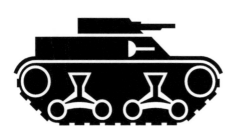

The Cold War

Mao: "What do breaking dishes and 1948 have in common?"
Chiang: "They both involve the fall of China."

Joe: "Which Cold War alliance was best prepared for a trip?"
Ivan: "I'm not sure about NATO, but Warsaw Pact."

Teacher: "How were our Marines able to protect the retreat from North Korea?"
Wiseguy: "We had a few well-Chosin defenders."

During the negotiations for the SALT Treaty Henry Kissinger peppered the Soviets with questions.

The test at Bikini Atoll got rather skimpy coverage in the press.

After the Bay of Pigs fiasco, Castro thought he could hog all of Cuba to himself.

I'm glad they changed the spelling of his name; Mao Tse Tung sounds like a Chinese delicacy.

When the North Vietnamese called for the complete withdrawal of all US forces unconditionally the US president said, 'Nixon that!"

I'll bet Henry wasn't very Fonda his daughter when she came out in support of the North Vietnamese.

Dick: "What did the residents say after the Communists changed the name of the Vietnamese capital to Ho Chi Minh City?"
Patricia: "Sigh, gone (Saigon) already."
Ronnie: "What was our best secret weapon during the Cold War?"
Nancy: "Our Reagan (ray gun)."

George: "Why did Reagan have so much difficulty negotiating with the USSR in his first term?"
Barbara: "The leaders died so often they would drop off, Andropov, Andropov."

Teacher: "Why did the leaders of the coup attempt against Gorbachev fail?"
Wiseguy: "Because its leaders turned out to be green instead of red!"

Teacher: "Why did the USSR break apart?"
Wiseguy: "Because Boris Yeltsin was Russian towards independence".

Gorby: "What do losing a board game and the end of the Cold War have in common?"
Raisa: "The Soviets couldn't keep their monopoly over the Baltic Avenue."

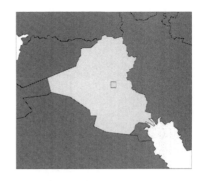

Recent times

First student: "I think we should have stayed out the first Gulf War."
Second student: "That Saddam idea if you ask me."
First student: "I'll bet you Kuwait to get started."
Second student: "Iraq my brains trying to think of a way out of it."
Third student: "Hussein we're going to win anyhow?"

Monica: "What did Hillary say when she kicked Bill in the rear?
Bubba: 'Intern? My turn. I feel your pain!'"

Donkey: "Why did you vote for George Bush?"
Elephant: "Because two Bushes in the White House is worth one Byrd in the Senate."

Clarence: "What do Muammar Qaddafi and the 2000 election have in common?"
Sandra: "Punching out a little Chad got them into a lot of trouble."

Ivan: "What happened when Boris Yeltsin was tired of being president?"
Natasha: "He decided to Putin a successor."

Eli: "How could you tell that Arafat surrounded himself with yes men?"
Jacob: "Every time he gave an order his followers said, 'Yasir, I can do that!'"

Librarian: "Which volume of the encyclopedia got used the most in the year 2000?"
Student: "Y to K." (Y2K)

Mac: "What do you get when you cross a former Israeli prime minister and an internet search engine?"
PC: "Netanyahoo."

Ever since the arrest of Saddam Hussein the fortunes of the Baath Party have really gone down the drain!

Chapter Three: Career Day

I wanted to be a (an)...

accountant, but it just didn't add up. I kept losing my balance and I just couldn't figure it out.

actor, but I didn't want to make a scene. Maybe I can stage a comeback.

archeologist, can you dig it? My love life was terrible; I tried to date everything I found.

architect, but it wasn't in the plans.

artist, but I wasn't good at canvassing.

automotive mechanic, but I wanted to get away from the 'hood.

baker, but I loafed around too much, and didn't make enough dough.

banker, but I lost interest in it.

boot maker, but I gave that up after much sole searching.

butcher, but I was a cut up.

carpenter, I thought I really nailed that one, but it soon it became the same old saw.

cave explorer, but I couldn't get into it. I made money, but just couldn't get out of the hole.

chemist, but it was too elementary for me. The work was really vial.

chiropractor, but I was a pain in the neck. Besides, it's not all its cracked up to be.

coach, but I tried another field.

cobbler, but I got tongue-tied. I was too straight-laced for that kind of work anyway.

computer hardware engineer, so I could be in the chips.

computer software engineer, but that was a baud idea.

cook in an East Indian restaurant, but I couldn't curry any favor. I'm really sari that didn't work out.

court reporter, but don't say that on the record.

dancer, but I couldn't get a leg up on the competition.

dentist, but it got me down in the mouth.

disc jockey, but it was a record-breaking moment.

doctor, but I had no patience (patients).

driver, no one was able to steer me in the right direction.

electrician, at first I got a charge out of it, but the risk was too shocking.

Besides, I was too wired all of the time.

elevator operator, but that has its ups and downs.

environmental scientist, but I was too green to have any experience at it.

exterminator, but I couldn't get all of the bugs out.

farmer, I saw a lot of growth potential in it. I wanted to get ahead in my field.

fireman, but I'm too burned out. My career is hosed.

fisherman, I got hooked on it. I like to work on the fly.

fitness worker, but it didn't work out. I'll have to exercise different options now.

gastrointestinal doctor, but I didn't have the guts for it.

golfer, I'd heard it was a fairway to make a living, but I couldn't get into the club. I couldn't get the swing of it, so I got teed off.

horse trainer, buy I didn't want to get saddled with that.

human resources assistant, but I just couldn't apply

myself.

hunter, but my career is shot.

janitor, I thought I could really clean up with that job!

laundry worker, but my career is washed up.

locksmith, but I got too keyed up about it.

landscape architect, I thought it was all laid out for me.

lawyer, but they kept raising the bar on me.

loan officer, no one would give me credit.

librarian, check it out!

lumberjack, but I think I'm barking up the wrong tree. Besides, I just ain't that sort of feller!

mail carrier, but I couldn't deliver.

mechanic, leaving that job was a gut wrenching decision.

miller, but I couldn't take the daily grind.

musician, but I didn't know the score.

nurse, but the cost of nursing school was off the charts.

pharmacist, yeah, they drug me into it.

photographer, but I couldn't picture it. I was too negative. I guess I'll wait to see if something better develops!

physicist, what's the matter with that?

pilot, but I crashed and burned.

plumber, but my career went down the drain. My job really gave me that sinking feeling.

police officer, yeah, that's the ticket!

politician, but I ran into a poll.

psychologist, but I couldn't wrap my head around that.

real estate agent, but never felt at home with that.

reporter, but that's another story.

river boat pilot, but someone steered me in a different direction.

roofer, but I got the shingles.

seamstress, but I hated that darn job. Besides, its not what it seems.

secretary, but I was type cast.

social worker, so get off my case!

statistician, what are the odds of that?

surveyor, but I didn't measure up to people's expectations.

tailor, but it was a sew-sew job.

teacher, but I have no class. Besides, I couldn't make the grade.

telephone operator, but I had too many hang-ups.

telemarketer, but it wasn't my calling.

typist, but I got too keyed up. Maybe I just needed to try a different shift.

urban planner, but I kept zoning out.

vacuum cleaner repairman, but it really sucked.

veterinarian, but my career went to the dogs.

weaver, but I was a knotty girl.

webmaster, but I kept losing a button, and then my career took too many hits. When I finally quit, it was very refreshing.

writer, but I decided to turn over a new page.

zookeeper, I was first in lion to get the job, but I couldn't bear the work.

Chapter Four: Famous Flubs

These are actual student answers on tests or papers. Whether they were trying to be intentionally funny or not I will leave up to you:

"The Italian unification movement was led by Gary Baldy."

"The Quakers were a group of people who invented Quakers Oats."

"The Aztecs were defeated by the Spanish because they were a nation of worriers."

"The organetto was an instrument which worked by blowing hot air through popes."

"Saddam Hussein built weapons of mass distraction."

"Massachusetts Bay Colony was a colony by Massachusetts Bay."

"The Puritans were a group of colonists who lived in the Southern colonies and invented a corn oil."

"King George III was the king of England during the Revolutionary War. He was a little looney toon."

"The Treaty of Paris said that all plaster must be purchased in Paris."

"The Battle of Bull Run was the way the cowboys chased the cattle to make them run."

"Hitler was the person most responsible for the end of the Cold War."

"The most famous battle with the Indians was called Knee High."

"The Nationalists were led by Chiang Kai Shrek."

"Israel has taken over the Golem Heights from Syria."

All-time worst student answer:
"The German he winned Werld War Too 'cuz the Untied State loosed it."

Some of the more notable things heard in class:

First Student: "Did we win WWII?"
Not-so-nice-neighbor: "Are you speaking German, dummy?"

Teacher: "Marx was the founder of Communism."
Pupil: "Groucho or Harpo?"

Teacher: "The Russian Revolution was lead by Lenin."
Student: "The guy in the Beatles?"
Another student: "What were the Beatles?"

Teacher: "Hitler was probably the worst dictator of all time."
Student: "Who was Hitler?"

Teacher: "Which Reformation leader was the most important after Martin Luther?"
Student: "Martin Luther King?"

Teacher: "Why do you think the United States won the Cold War?"
Student: "Wait a minute, we won the Cold War? What

happened to the Soviet Union?"

Teacher: "The dictator Tito ruled Yugoslavia from the end of WWII to his death in 1980."
Student: "Michael Jackson's brother?"

Teacher: "The Madonna and child is one of the most prevalent images in art."
Student: "She has a kid? I thought she divorced Sean Penn."

Teacher: "Do you think Hillary will run for president?"
Student: "Hillary Duff?"

Record any of your own jokes or famous flubs here:

How to contact the author:

It is my sincere hope that you will find these jokes as enjoyable, educational, and student-engaging as I have. Should you feel like you need further information or have suggestions for this book, our simulations or other books, please contact me via e-mail at:
Krinibar@aol.com
or via US Mail at:
Richard Di Giacomo
2486 Aram Avenue
San Jose, California 95128 USA

Or visit our webpage at http://www.magnificopublications.com

HOW TO ORDER:

*M*agnifico *P*ublications *O*rder *F*orm

(1) Order our books through our web page at
http://www.magnificopublications.com.
(2) Order them through the following web pages:
Social Studies School Services. www.socialstudies.com/
http://www.amazon.com/, Google Play or www.Dedicatedteacher.com
(3) Contact Magnifico Publications directly at (408) 286-5179 or e-mail us
at krinibar@aol.com.
(4) Mail this order form to: *Magnifico Publications*   2486 Aram Ave. San
Jose, CA. 95128. Ship to:

Name_____
School or
Organization_____
Department:_____
Address_____
City_____
State_____ZIP_____
Country_____
E-Mail Address_____
Phone (_____)_____

Title(s):   cost:

ISBN-13 978-0-9706237-2-0   *The New Man and the New World:*
The Influence of Renaissance Humanism on the Explorers of the Italian Era of
Discovery   15.95
ISBN-13 978-0-9706237-3-7   *The History Teacher's Joke Book*   9.99

ISBN-13 978-0-9706237-6-8   *Ohlone Teacher's Resource Book*   25.00
ISBN-13 978-0-9706237-7-5   *The History Teacher's Movie Guide Choosing*
and Using the Right Films for Your Classroom   17.50
ISBN-13 978-0-9706237-8-2 *When Am I Ever Going to Use This Stuff*   17.50
ISBN-13 978-0-9834267-1-4   *Tales of Time*   19.99
ISBN-13 978-0-9853006-7-8 *Historical Gems of the San Francisco Bay Area*
                                                                   20.00

Subtotal   _____
Shipping & handling   6.00
Tax (CA only)   _____
Total   _____

NOTE: The following titles, formerly distributed by Magnifico Publications, are now available in expanded and revised editions from Interact, the first name in social studies simulations. NOTE: The following titles, formerly distributed by Magnifico Publications, are now available in expanded and revised editions from Interact, the first name in social studies simulations. See www.socialstudies.com for ordering information:

ISBN-13 978-0-9706237-9-9 Creative Geography Activities for the 21st Century

ISBN-13 978-0-9834267-3-8 Short Role-playing Simulations for US History Classrooms ISBN-13 978-0-9706237-5-1 US History Activities for English Language Learners ISBN-13 978-0-9834267-2-1 Short Role-playing Simulations for World History Classrooms

ISBN-13 978-0-9834267-4-5 Short Role-playing Simulations for Middle School World History

ISBN-13 978-0-9834267-0-7 Short Role-playing Simulations for Early US History

Made in the USA
Lexington, KY
02 June 2017